ENTERING
EST. ♡ 1690
ROCKPORT

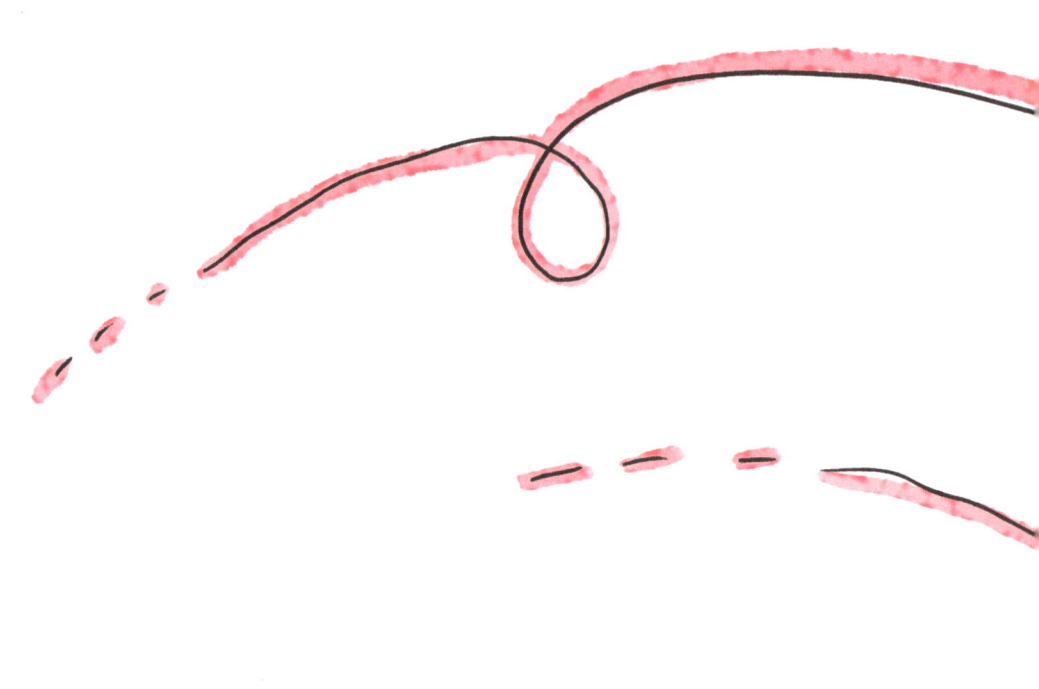

Copyright © 2022 Ruth L. Fritz
ISBN: 978-1-7364706-19
Printed and published by Amazon Kindle Direct Publishing
and Ingram Spark

Copyright notice: All rights reserved. No portion of this book may be reproduced in any form without permission from the publisher, except as permitted by U.S. copyright law.

This is a work of creative nonfiction. Any resemblance to actual persons, living or dead, or actual events is either purely coincidental or the relevant persons have given permission for their likenesses to appear.

Design and Illustration: Elizabeth DiFiore
Color Assistance: Veronica Mills

Kisses from Rockport

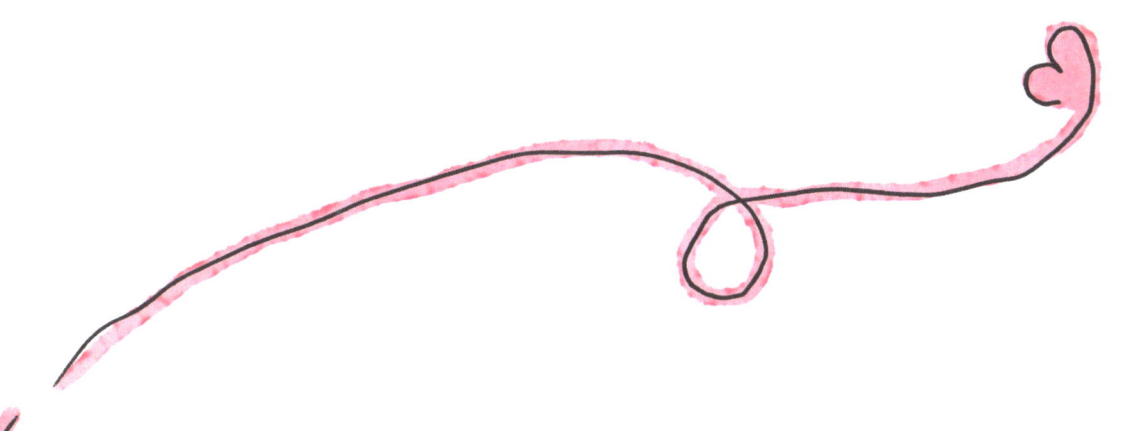

DEDICATION
To children everywhere,
may you feel love.

This is a story about a wonderful boy named Matthew and his equally wonderful sister, Katelyn.

They live with their Mom and Dad and their very fluffy dog, Mookie.

Matthew and Katelyn usually get along very well.

But, one particular Monday they had a BIG disagreement!

Matthew and Katelyn have grandparents, Nana and Papa, who live an hour away in a beautiful town by the sea called Rockport.

When Matthew and Katelyn were very young, Nana and Papa got up very, very early, before the sun woke up, and drove to Sudbury to take care of them while their parents were at work.

Mondays were always lots of fun.

The day started with dancing!

Matthew and Katelyn loved to cook. The toy kitchen had lots of pots and pans and make believe food. Matthew put on his chef's hat and cooked and Katelyn served wearing her favorite tutu.

Nana and Papa thought the food was "deeelicious," but Matthew always had Katelyn bring it back because it needed "more garlic!"

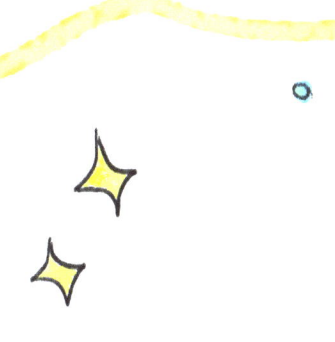

Katelyn loved to play with her dolls.
There were many to dress and feed.

Sometimes Katelyn, Matthew, Nana and Papa would take the dolls in their doll-carriage on long walks through the neighborhood...

Well... all except Aweegie.

Aweegie had very short hair that Katelyn had cut all by herself! And, Aweegie had freckles all over her face that Katelyn had made with a blue pen!

According to Katelyn, Aweegie doesn't behave very well, so she often couldn't go for walks because she was in time-out.

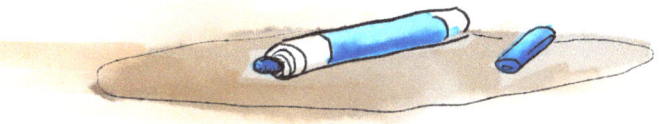

There were lots of Monday outings to the local farms, orchards, playgrounds, and picnic spots.

Searching for construction sites to watch diggers and dump trucks was exciting too.

On rainy days it was fun to go to the local bagel shop where they enjoyed music and a children's sing-along in the afternoon.

Matthew brought his little red guitar and Katelyn brought her flowered maracas.

When day was done Matthew and Katelyn got ready for bed. Matthew tucked his best buddy, Bunny, into his bed.

Katelyn picked out special dolls and stuffed animals for cuddling. But, before they got into bed themselves, it was time to say goodbye to Nana and Papa.

With pjs on, they ran to the door and got big goodbye hugs and kisses.

As Matthew and Katelyn stood by the door waving, Nana always called back to them, "I'll blow you kisses from Rockport."

As Nana and Papa drove home to Rockport they always talked about their special Monday with Matthew and Katelyn and how much fun they had.

When Nana finally got to lay her head on her pillow, as promised, she blew a kiss to Matthew and to Katelyn and whispered, "I love you!"

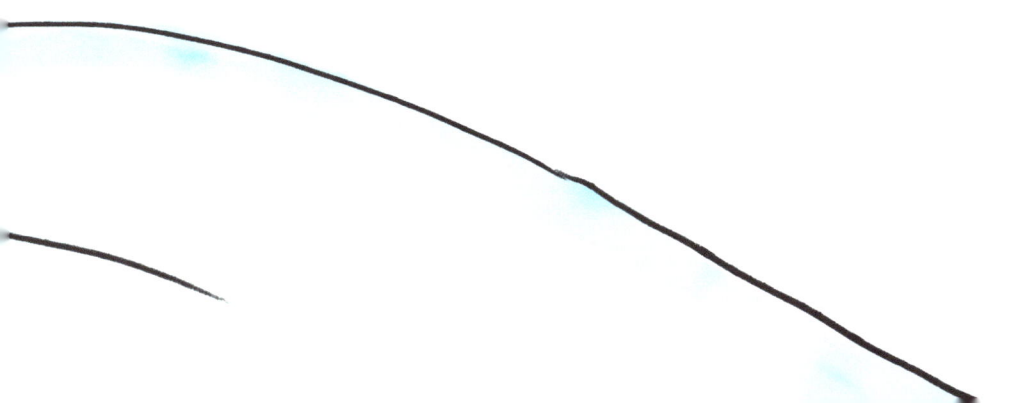

A few years passed and Matthew and Katelyn were a little older now.

Nana and Papa were happy to still have their special Mondays with them.

As always, with each goodbye Nana stood by the car and promised to blow kisses from Rockport.

Katelyn immediately became upset at Matthew and yelled at him, "Yes she can! It is real!" They argued back and forth.

Matthew finally asked Katelyn, "How do you know it's real?"

And Katelyn in her most serious and confident voice said, "Because I can feel it!"

Nana didn't go right home to Rockport that Monday night. She went back into the house and sat down with Matthew and Katelyn. Nana explained to both of them that what Katelyn was describing was the feeling of love.

Nana said, "Love is something you can feel even when you can't see it.
It's like the sun and the wind and the air we breathe... you know it's there."

Many more years have passed since that night. Matthew and Katelyn are much older now. Nana and Papa don't go to Sudbury every Monday anymore.

But, whenever they spend time with Matthew and Katelyn, it's still very, very special.

And when it's time for Nana and Papa to go home to Rockport, Matthew and Katelyn are **now** the ones who say to Nana, "Blow us kisses from Rockport."

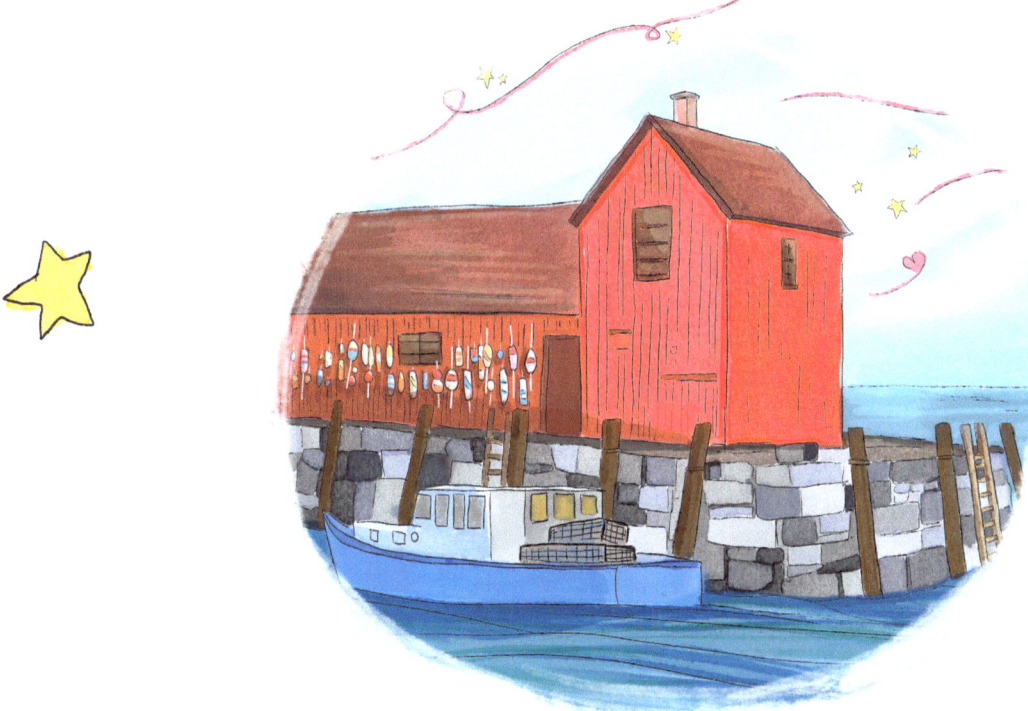

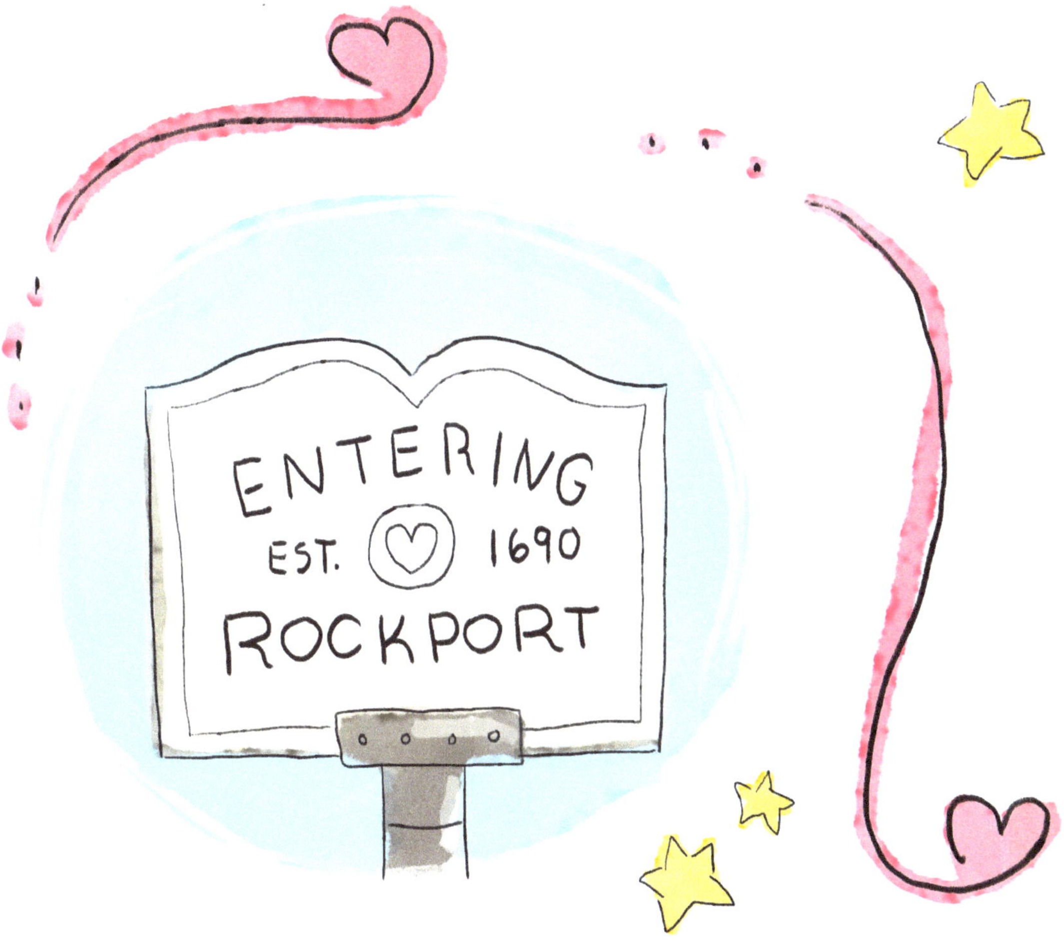
ENTERING
EST. 1690
ROCKPORT

About The Author

Dr. Ruth Fritz is a clinical psychologist and clinical nurse specialist in psychiatric-mental health. She has three grown children and two grandchildren, Matthew and Katelyn. She lives in Rockport, MA with her adorable Havanese, Gracie, and her adorable husband, John.

www.ingramcontent.com/pod-product-compliance
Lightning Source LLC
LaVergne TN
LVHW072118070426
835510LV00003B/107